SWEET DREAMS

RECIPES FOR DELIGHTFUL INDULGENCES

C.R.Gibson®

FINE.GIFTS SINCE 1870

Recipes

A classic collection of recipes is provided in this international repertoire of cakes, ranging from the Italian Certosino and Biscuit de Savoie from France, to Mississippi Mud Pie from North America – all complete with introductory material. The mouth-watering collection of delicious cakes includes recipes for all occasions, and there is something here to please everyone.

An indulgence prepared in one's kitchen is doubly delightful and doubly satisfying.

Flans & Tarts

A 13th-century Arab manuscript describes a tart filled with a syrupy nut, date, and poppy seed mixture, flavored with rose water, tinted with saffron, and cooked with a roasting chicken suspended above, dripping juices onto the tart. Today flans and tarts excite in a more familiar way. Crisp pastry encases jewel-like berries or citrus slices. Caramelized fruit juices and vanilla creams enhance the flavor and nuts give texture.

French Flan with Red Berries

Rings of colorful, fresh summer berries over a rich and creamy filling within a sweet pastry case look attractive and tempting.

A feast for the eyes, bursts of fruity flavors for the mouth …

— *Making the Flan* —

Flavor the crème pâtissière with fresh vanilla if you can. It has a much more subtle and delicate flavor than vanilla extract and the bean can be rinsed off, allowed to dry, and saved for another occasion.

INGREDIENTS

For the flan case

1 quantity
sweet flan pastry

For the filling

2 tbsp apricot jam, sieved

1 quantity crème pâtissière
(pastry cream)

1½ pints (750ml) strawberries,
raspberries, and blueberries or other
soft fruit

For the decoration

1 quantity
red currant glaze

confectioners' sugar

1 Allow the pastry to come back to room temperature. Knead briefly until smooth, roll out on a lightly floured surface, and use to line the prepared pan. Chill for 1 hour.

2 Prick the bottom all over with a fork and bake with pie weights in the preheated oven for 10 minutes. Remove the pie weights and bake for 10–15 minutes longer, or until it is crisp and golden. Remove from the oven and let cool on a wire rack.

3 Brush the pastry case with the apricot jam. Spoon in the crème pâtissière and spread evenly over the base with a small narrow spatula or the back of a spoon. Arrange the prepared fruit close together in concentric circles over the top of the crème pâtissière.

4 Spoon the red currant glaze evenly over the fruit up to the edge of the pastry so that it forms a seal, and let set. Take out of the pan, transfer to a serving plate, and dust the edges of the pastry lightly with confectioners' sugar just before serving.

Oven temperature
400°F/200°C

Baking time
20–25 minutes

Tart pan
9in (23cm) fluted tart
pan, greased

Makes
8 slices

Storage
Keeps for 1–2 days

... the tart is a complete sensory experience.

Special Ingredients

Mixed berries such as blueberries, raspberries, and strawberries are deliciously sweet yet tart in flavor. They taste best when picked fully ripe. Wash them briefly with their stems intact to retain errant juices, then dry on paper towels. They should not be sugared.

Blueberries

Raspberries

Vanilla beans give the crème pâtissière its wonderful flavor.

Strawberries

Pies & Tarts

Fill a crisp pastry shell or crunchy cookie crust with sumptuous chocolate to create a perfect dessert combination. There are so many delectable choices, from Chocolate Pear Tart, in which the fruit enhances the taste of the chocolate, to light-as-air Chocolate

Chiffon Pie topped with swirls of whipped cream, and a chocolate-rich version of Banoffee Pie. Ice cream and whipped cream, the classic accompaniments for dessert pies, are particularly apt when served with chocolate, for they intensify its unique flavor.

Mississippi Mud Pie

A favorite recipe in the American South, this pie has a luscious chocolate filling, with a dash of coffee flavoring, enclosed in a light egg pastry shell.

INGREDIENTS

For the pastry shell

1 quantity sweet shortcrust pastry

For the filling

10 tbsp (150g) butter
1oz (30g) semisweet chocolate, chopped
6 tbsp (45g) cocoa powder, sifted
2 tsp instant espresso coffee powder
3 eggs
1 cup (250g) superfine sugar
2 tbsp sour cream
3 tbsp corn syrup
1 tsp vanilla extract
white, milk, and semisweet chocolate curls, to decorate

1 Allow the pastry to come to room temperature. Knead it briefly, then roll it out on a lightly floured surface. Use the pastry to line the prepared 9in (23cm)-diameter, loose-based tart pan, rolling it out quite thinly. Chill the pastry shell while preparing the filling.

2 Put a baking sheet in the lower third of the oven and preheat the oven.

3 For the filling, gently melt the butter in a small saucepan. Remove from the heat and stir in the chocolate, cocoa powder, and coffee, stirring until the chocolate has melted. Set aside.

4 Beat the eggs and sugar together until the mixture is creamy and blended, then add the sour cream, corn syrup, and vanilla extract. Stir in the chocolate and butter mixture.

5 Pour the filling into the pastry shell. Bake on the hot baking sheet in the preheated oven for 35–40 minutes, or until the filling puffs up and forms a crust. Remove the pie to a wire rack to cool. The filling will sink a little and may crack slightly as it cools.

6 Before serving, decorate the pie with chocolate curls: a mixture of different colored curls looks impressive. Vanilla ice cream is an excellent accompaniment for this pie.

Oven temperature
350°F/180°C

Baking time
35–40 minutes

Baking pan
1½in (3.5cm)-deep, 9in (23cm)-diameter, loose-based tart pan, greased

Makes
8–10 slices

Storage
Keeps for 2 days in the refrigerator

T raffitional desserts from the deep South are as rich and dark as the soil along the Mississippi delta.

MISSISSIPPI MUD PIE
This richly dark pie has a wonderfully smooth filling, containing two kinds of chocolate baked in a sweet pastry shell. Elegant chocolate curls complete a memorable dessert pie.

Large chocolate curls make a stylish topping

The sweet, creamy filling gives this pie its name

Butter Cakes

Simple butter cakes are very easy to make. They are based on a combination of the key cake ingredients: butter, sugar, eggs, and flour, in varying proportions. These plain, tasty cakes are satisfyingly rich with a buttery texture and excellent flavor, ideal for serving with a cup of coffee in the afternoon or after dinner. Although they are not elaborate, the addition of special ingredients such as chocolate, fresh fruit, spices, or nuts, together with a coating of sweet glacé icing, readily transforms them into memorable treats.

Pound Cake

In her 1747 book, The Art of Cookery Made Plain and Easy, *Hannah Glasse explained how to "Make a Pound Cake" using a pound of flour, a pound of butter, a pound of sugar, eight eggs and "a great wooden Spoon." Today we no longer have to make such large quantities or rely on the spoon – using a machine makes much lighter work.*

INGREDIENTS

1 cup (125g) all-purpose flour, sifted
¼ cup (125g) potato starch
1 tsp baking powder
1 cup (250g) butter
1 cup plus 2 tbsp (250g) granulated sugar
seeds from ¼ of a vanilla bean
4 large eggs
1 tsp finely grated lemon zest
1 tbsp milk
confectioners' sugar to decorate

1 Sift the all-purpose flour, potato starch, and baking powder together. Set aside. Beat the butter, sugar, and vanilla seeds together until pale and fluffy. Beat in the eggs, one at a time, adding a little of the flour if the mixture begins to separate. Beat in the lemon zest.

2 Gradually beat in the flour until everything is evenly mixed. Stir in the milk. Spoon the mixture into the prepared pan and bake in the preheated oven for 1 hour, or until a fine skewer inserted into the cake comes out clean.

3 Remove the cake from the oven, ease away from the sides of the pan, and let rest for 10 minutes. Invert onto a wire rack and let cool. Transfer to a plate and dust with confectioners' sugar.

VARIATIONS

Fresh Fruit Pound Cake
Make the basic mixture, omitting the milk. Pit and roughly chop ¾lb (350g) apricots, apples, plums, or peaches into ½in (1cm) pieces. Stir in 1 tablespoon lemon juice and fold the fruit into the basic mixture. Bake for 1¼ hours. Decorate with 1 quantity lemon glacé icing (see page 30) and fine lemon shreds once cold.

Chocolate Marble Pound Cake
Make the basic mixture, omitting the milk. Put half into another bowl and stir in 2 tablespoons cocoa powder blended with 2 tablespoons dark rum and 2½oz (75g) melted semisweet chocolate. Drop alternating spoonfuls of each mixture into the prepared pan and bake for 1 hour. Decorate with 1 quantity chocolate glacé icing (see page 30) once cold.

Mixed Spice Pound Cake
Sift 1 teaspoon ground cinnamon and ½ teaspoon grated nutmeg with the flour. Fold into the basic mixture with ¼ cup (60g) chopped toasted hazelnuts. Bake for 1 hour. Decorate with granulated sugar, cinnamon, and chopped hazelnuts once cold.

Oven temperature
350°F/180°C

Baking time
1 hour; 1¼ hours for the fresh fruit cakes

Cake pan
5 cup (1.5 liter) bundt pan, greased twice with melted butter and floured

Makes
12–16 slices

Storage
Fruit cakes keep for 2–3 days; others for 5–6 days

BASIC POUND CAKE *liberally dusted with confectioners' sugar.*

CHOCOLATE MARBLE POUND CAKE *topped with a chocolate glacé icing.*

MIXED SPICE POUND CAKE *decorated with cinnamon, sugar, and hazelnuts.*

FRESH APRICOT POUND CAKE *crowned with glacé icing and lemon shreds.*

A staple for more than 4000 years, easily digested, and filled with vitamins A & D, butter is a rare combination – an ingredient that is both nutritious and delicious.

Dessert Cakes

Single-layer cakes make fine dessert cakes, especially good when served with a sauce, such as crème anglaise, or a fruit coulis or syrup, like the kumquat syrup made for the Celestial Kumquat Torte on this page. Many dessert cakes are in the rich tradition of the Austrian and German torte, often enriched with nuts or seeds and containing little or no flour. The classic Sacher Torte is among such cakes, as well as Torta di Castagne e Cioccolato, a delicious Italian cake that combines chocolate with chestnuts.

Celestial Kumquat Torte

INGREDIENTS

For the kumquats

1lb (500g) kumquats
½ cup (150g) granulated sugar
1¼ cups (300ml) water

For the cake

⅓ cup (45g) self-rising cake flour
½ cup (150g) superfine sugar
pinch of salt
3 eggs
3oz (90g) bittersweet chocolate
1 tbsp cocoa powder
7 tbsp (100g) unsalted butter

For the glaze

4oz (125g) semisweet chocolate
2 tbsp unsalted butter
2 tbsp milk
chocolate leaves, to decorate

Kumquats, a native of China introduced into the United States in about 1850, are closely related to citrus fruits but, uniquely, have a sweet edible rind. The sharp yet sweet flavor of poached kumquats and their syrup goes well with many chocolate desserts, including this rich torte.

1 Wash the kumquats and halve them lengthwise, leaving 9–10 whole for decoration. Put in a pan with the sugar and water. Bring to a boil and cook very slowly for 30 minutes, until soft. Set aside.

2 For the cake, put the flour, sugar, salt, and eggs in a large bowl set over hot but not boiling water and beat with an electric beater for 8 minutes. The mixture should become very thick and leave a ribbon trail when the beater is lifted.

3 Melt the chocolate, cocoa powder, and butter together. Add to the egg mixture and beat for a few minutes. Pour the mixture into the prepared pan and bake in the preheated oven for 25 minutes, or until the cake is springy to the touch. Remove from the oven and run a knife around the inside edge of the pan. Leave for 10 minutes before turning out onto a wire rack.

4 Melt the glaze ingredients together. Put the cake, on the wire rack, on a plate to catch excess glaze. Cool the glaze slightly so it thickens, then pour it over the warm cake, spreading it evenly with a narrow spatula. Leave for 10 minutes to set.

5 Decorate the top with chocolate leaves and the whole kumquats and serve the cake lukewarm, with the remaining kumquats and syrup.

Oven temperature
325°F/160°C

Baking time
25 minutes

Baking pan
8in (20cm) springform pan, greased and lined on the bottom

Makes
8–10 slices

Storage
Keeps for 2–3 days in the refrigerator

Festival Cakes

Preparing a cake for a special occasion, whether religious or secular, has long been a ritual. As a result, many rich and luxurious recipes have passed from generation to generation. Indeed, the tradition of baking has its origins in the feasts and festivals of the distant past – spices, dried fruit, and nuts, which were once coveted and costly ingredients, were reserved especially for such times.

THE CAKE'S TEXTURE *is dense and honey-enriched, studded with nuts and dried fruit, and lightly marbled with chocolate.*

Certosino

Special Ingredients

Golden raisins can be plumped up in hot water for 30 minutes before using.

Dark rum imparts rich, sweet moisture.

Honey with a fine aroma and clear tones makes the best sweetener.

Cinnamon adds an intense aromatic taste.

Aniseed gives the cake its distinctive licorice flavor.

Apple purée adds a moist, rich texture.

Candied fruit, walnuts, and pecans are traditional festive decorations.

Almonds are blanched in boiling water, then sliced into thin flakes.

Semisweet chocolate must be high in cocoa fat for a good flavor.

Pine nuts have a mild but delicious resinous flavor.

Making the Cake

This is a traditional Italian Christmas cake that originated with the Carthusian monks of Bologna during medieval times. It is decorated with a sumptuous assortment of nuts and candied fruit.

INGREDIENTS

For the cake

½ cup (75g) golden raisins
1½ tbsp dark rum
1½ cups (350g) honey
3 tbsp butter
3 tbsp water
2 tsp aniseed
scant 3¼ cups (400g) all-purpose flour
1½ tsp baking soda
1 tsp ground cinnamon
¾ cup (400g) apple purée
1½ cups (180g) blanched almonds, coarsely chopped or sliced
2½ oz (75g) semisweet chocolate, coarsely chopped
¾ cup (180g) candied orange and lemon peel, finely chopped
3 tbsp pine nuts

For the decoration

3 tbsp apricot glaze
1½–2lb (750g–1kg) candied fruit, candied peel, walnut or pecan halves

1 For the cake, put the golden raisins and rum in a small bowl. Cover with plastic wrap and let soak for 30 minutes.

2 Put the honey, butter, and water together in a heavy-bottomed pan. Set over low heat and leave until melted. Stir in the aniseed.

3 Sift the flour, baking soda, and cinnamon into a large bowl. Slowly pour in the honey mixture and mix thoroughly until smooth. Stir in the apple purée, almonds, chocolate, candied peel, rum-soaked golden raisins, and pine nuts.

4 Spoon the mixture into the prepared pan and bake in the preheated oven for 1 hour–1 hour 10 minutes. Remove from the oven and invert onto a wire rack. Peel off the lining paper and let cool.

5 To decorate, brush the top of the cake with half the apricot glaze. Arrange the candied fruit, candied peel, and nuts decoratively over the cake and then brush once more with the remaining glaze. Let set before serving or storing.

Oven temperature
325°F/160°C

Baking time
1 hour–1 hour 10 minutes

Cake pan
9in (23cm) springform pan, greased and lined

Makes
16 slices

Storage
Keeps for 1 week

A cake from the store is just a cake; a cake prepared in your kitchen becomes an exquisite gift for a friend or loved one.

Rich Layer Cakes

Layer cakes, richly filled and sumptuously decorated, tempt the eye as well as the taste buds. Layer cakes range from the light sponge of the airy-textured Gâteau Royale to the intensely dark Pecan Chocolate Fudge Cake. In some cakes, the layers are not so obvious: two roulades turn single layers of cake into wheels within wheels, and a pound cake twists chocolate and vanilla layers into each other for a marbled effect. The ultimate layer cake is a beribboned, three-tiered Wedding Cake.

Chocolate Layer Cake

A very quick and easy cake to make and one of my family's favorites. The cake, which has the texture of a firm brownie, is sliced into thin layers, sandwiched together with whipped cream.

INGREDIENTS

For the cake

½ cup (125g) unsalted butter
½ cup (60g) cocoa powder, sifted
2 eggs
1 cup (250g) superfine sugar
1 tsp vanilla extract
½ cup (60g) all-purpose flour
½ cup (60g) self-rising flour

For the filling and decoration

2 tbsp milk
2 cups (450ml) heavy cream
2 tbsp superfine sugar
½ tsp vanilla extract
semisweet chocolate curls

1 Melt the butter in a saucepan over low heat, then stir in the cocoa until blended. Set aside. Beat the eggs with the sugar and vanilla until light, then stir in the cocoa mixture.

2 Sift the flours together twice. Sift them over the egg mixture, a third at a time, folding each one in with a metal spoon. Turn into the prepared pan and bake in the preheated oven for 40–45 minutes, or until a skewer inserted in the center comes out clean.

3 Run a knife around the inside edge of the pan and leave the cake for 10 minutes before turning out onto a wire rack to cool completely. When the cake is cold, wrap it in foil and chill overnight. Although this is not absolutely necessary, it makes the cake easier to slice.

4 With the cake at room temperature, cut it into four equal layers, using a long serrated knife. The cake layers will be very thin, so use two narrow spatulas to move them.

5 For the filling, add the milk to the cream and whip until it forms soft peaks. Fold in the sugar and vanilla.

6 Use the top layer, cut side up, as the base. Cover it with some of the cream. Add a second layer and cover with cream; repeat with a third layer. Finish with the bottom layer, cut side down. Cover the top and sides of the cake with the remaining cream and decorate with chocolate curls.

VARIATION

Chocolate Praline Layer Cake
Use 1 quantity praline (see page 30). Fold 8 tablespoons (120g) praline into two-thirds of the whipped cream. Use the plain whipped cream for one layer and the praline cream for two. Cover the top and sides of the cake with the rest of the praline cream. Use the remaining praline to coat the sides of the cake. Decorate the top with chocolate curls.

Oven temperature
350°F/180°C

Baking time
40–45 minutes

Baking pan
8in (20cm) cake pan, greased and bottom-lined

Makes
8–10 slices

Storage
Unfilled cake keeps for 4–5 days, wrapped, in the refrigerator; filled cake keeps for 3 days in the refrigerator

CHOCOLATE PRALINE LAYER CAKE
Almond praline adds a sophisticated touch to the Chocolate Layer Cake.

Layer cakes require an architect's understanding of structure, an artist's talent for style, and a gourmand's cultured sense of taste.

Sponge Cakes

Sponge *biskuit* appeared in European cookery manuscripts as early as the mid-16th century, sometimes softly textured but often like a hard cookie. The egg mixture was usually heated, then tediously whipped to cool it down. Today, the cold method, which uses separated eggs, takes much less time, and the sponge cake remains a favorite in any cook's repertoire. Its light and airy structure gives a delicious background for soft fruit and whipped cream, for aromatic spices, nutty textures, and fruity spirits, and of course, for chocolate.

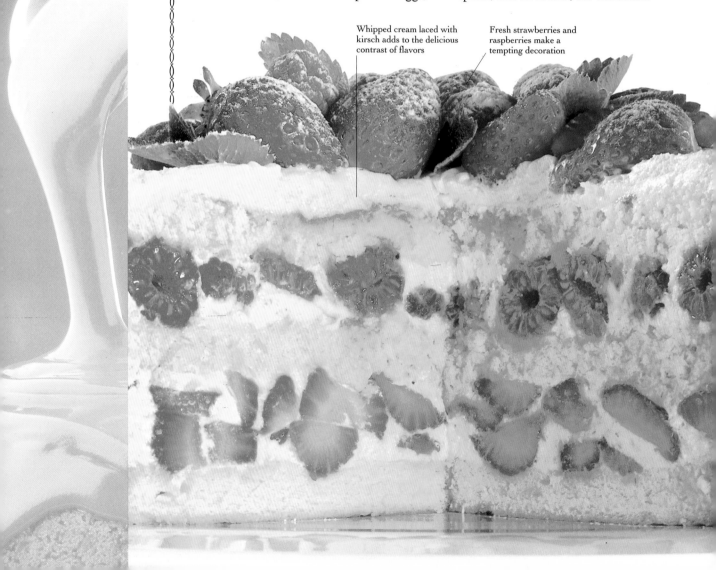

Whipped cream laced with kirsch adds to the delicious contrast of flavors

Fresh strawberries and raspberries make a tempting decoration

Biscuit de Savoie

In France, Germany, and Austria, biscuit is the usual name for light sponge cakes. Potato starch and eggs are the key ingredients for producing this light, airy mixture. It is especially suitable for layer and rolled cakes that require a firmer and slightly drier sponge.

INGREDIENTS

For the cake

²/₃ cup (60g) all-purpose flour
½ cup (60g) potato starch
2 cups (180g) confectioners' sugar, sifted
5 eggs, separated
pinch of salt
2 tsp lemon juice
½ tsp orange-flower water or 1 tsp dark rum

For the filling and decoration

6 tbsp (90ml) kirsch-flavored syrup
1 pint (500ml) fresh strawberries
½ pint (250ml) fresh raspberries
4 tbsp granulated sugar
1¼ cups (450ml) heavy cream
1 tbsp kirsch
strawberry leaves and confectioners' sugar

1 For the cake, sift the flour and potato starch together three times. Set aside.

2 Reserve 3 tablespoons of the confectioners' sugar. Whisk the remaining sugar and the egg yolks together to the ribbon stage.

3 In another bowl, whisk the egg whites and salt into soft peaks. Sift over the reserved sugar and whisk until they form slightly stiffer peaks. Fold in the lemon juice.

4 Stir 2 large spoonfuls of the egg white into the egg yolk mixture to loosen the texture. Gently fold in the flour and the orange-flower water or rum. Carefully fold in the remaining egg whites, taking care not to deflate the whites.

5 Pour the mixture into the prepared pan and bake in the center of the preheated oven for 35–40 minutes, or until a skewer comes out clean.

6 Remove from the oven and let rest in the pan for 5–10 minutes. Turn out onto a wire rack and let cool. Peel off the lining paper once cold.

TO FINISH THE CAKE

1 Slice the cake horizontally into three layers. Sprinkle the bottom two layers with the kirsch-flavored syrup. Place the bottom layer on a serving plate, syrup side up.

2 Set aside a few of the best strawberries and raspberries for the decoration. Remove the stems from the remaining strawberries and cut them into quarters. Mix the raspberries with 1 tablespoon of the granulated sugar. Whip the remaining sugar, the cream, and the kirsch into stiff peaks.

3 Carefully spoon the quartered strawberries evenly over the bottom cake layer, to within ⅓in (1cm) of the edge. Spoon over one third of the whipped cream and spread evenly over the fruit. Cover with the second syrup-soaked cake layer, syrup side up. Spoon over the raspberries and spread out, followed by another third of the cream. Cover with the top cake layer and press it down lightly so that the fruit becomes embedded in the cream.

4 For the decoration, spread the remaining cream evenly over the top of the cake, using a metal spatula. Arrange the reserved whole berries in the center, and decorate with the leaves. Dust with confectioners' sugar just before serving.

BISCUIT DE SAVOIE combines delicate sponge, kirsch-flavored cream, and juicy summer berries.

Oven temperature	350°F/180°C
Baking time	35–40 minutes
Cake pan	8½in (22cm) springform pan, greased and lined
Makes	8–10 slices
Storage	Keeps for 2–3 days in the refrigerator
Freezing	Freezes for 1 month, undecorated

Soft as a cushion or firm as a bed, the sponge cake can be perfectly adapted for any fruity topping or whipped embellishment.

Hot Chocolate Desserts

What could be better to take the chill out of a cold winter's day than a hot chocolate dessert? The aroma of chocolate wafting through the air arouses the taste buds to the joy of what's to come. There are a number of delightful winter warmers to tempt the palate, from a light, airy soufflé to a sumptuous, orange-scented steamed pudding. For a special occasion, you might consider elegant, thin crepes filled with luscious chocolate cream, or an aromatic rum-flavored chocolate fondue. All warming desserts for a winter treat.

Chocolate Rum Fondue

A very satisfying dessert for chocoholics. Place the warm chocolate fondue in the center of the table with a large platter of cake, cookies, freshly prepared fruit, and forks for dipping. The fondue can be flavored with any liqueur or left plain.

INGREDIENTS

½ cup (125g) superfine sugar
½ cup (125ml) water
6oz (180g) bittersweet chocolate
4 tbsp butter
¼ cup (50ml) rum
pound, angel food, or plain cake cut into 1in (2.5cm) cubes
ladyfingers or other plain cookies
fresh whole strawberries, small wedges of fresh pineapple or pear, orange segments, cherries, kiwifruit, and other fresh fruit

Serve an eye-catching display of fruits, cakes, and cookies for dipping into the fondue

1 Put the sugar and water in a saucepan and stir over low heat until the sugar has dissolved. Remove from the heat and set aside to cool.

2 Melt the chocolate with the butter. Stir the chocolate into the sugar syrup.

3 To serve, reheat the fondue in a microwave or in the top of a double boiler set over hot water. Stir the rum into the chocolate. Pour into a fondue pot or chafing dish. Serve the fondue warm, with fruits, cookies, and cubes of cake.

NOTE: The chocolate may have to be gently reheated halfway through. If you use a fondue pot or chafing dish with an alcohol burner, do not keep it on all the time as the chocolate can overheat, becoming grainy.

 Makes
6–8 servings

Storage
Keeps for 2 days in the refrigerator

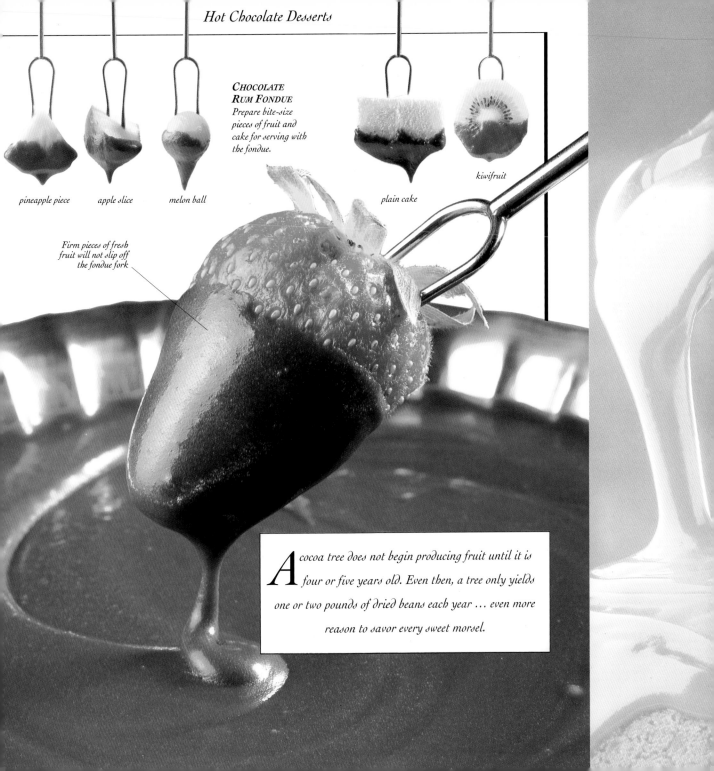

pineapple piece

apple slice

melon ball

CHOCOLATE RUM FONDUE
Prepare bite-size pieces of fruit and cake for serving with the fondue.

plain cake

kiwifruit

Firm pieces of fresh fruit will not slip off the fondue fork

A cocoa tree does not begin producing fruit until it is four or five years old. Even then, a tree only yields one or two pounds of dried beans each year ... even more reason to savor every sweet morsel.

Pastries & Cookies

Homemade pastries and cookies always add a welcoming note to any invitation for tea or coffee. Serve crisp-baked, toffeelike wafers full of nuts and glacé fruit, light and crunchy sugar cookies rich in butter, crisp cream puffs filled with fresh berries nestling in softly whipped cream, and wafer-thin almond cookies shaped like curved roof tiles. These delectable mouthfuls of sweet refreshment are always appreciated and hard to resist, so be sure to make plenty. If there are any left, store them in an airtight container.

A SELECTION OF
*Butter Cookies,
Florentines, and
Bienenstich*

Florentines

Florentines are a luxurious version of the old-fashioned brandy snap. Crisp and lacy, they can be coated with melted chocolate – semisweet, milk, or white. Mark the chocolate lightly with a fork if you want the cookies to look a little more fancy. Bake no more than five cookies at a time and watch them carefully; they burn very easily.

INGREDIENTS

¼ cup (90g) sliced almonds

¼ cup (30g) unblanched almonds, coarsely chopped

¼ cup (45g) candied orange and lemon peel, finely chopped

½ cup (30g) glacé cherries, washed, dried, and cut into small pieces

1 tbsp angelica, washed, dried, and cut into small pieces (optional)

1 tbsp all-purpose flour

scant ½ cup (100g) butter

scant ½ cup (100g) granulated sugar

2 tbsp clear honey

2 tbsp heavy cream

7oz (200g) semisweet chocolate, melted to decorate

1 Mix together the sliced and chopped almonds, peel, glacé cherries, angelica, and flour.

2 Put the butter, sugar, honey, and cream in a pan. Heat gently to dissolve the sugar. Bring to a boil and cook to 250°F/120°C.

3 Stir in the fruit and nut mixture and cook, stirring, for 1 minute, until the mixture rolls off the sides of the pan. Remove from the heat.

4 Drop 5 rounded teaspoons of the mixture 3in (7cm) apart on the prepared baking sheet and flatten each to a circle about 2½in (6cm) in diameter with the back of the spoon. Bake in the preheated oven for 8–10 minutes, until the edges are golden.

5 Remove from the oven and let cool for 3 minutes. Transfer to a wire rack with a metal spatula. Spread the back of each cookie with some of the melted chocolate and refrigerate to set.

Oven temperature
350°F/180°C

Baking time
8–10 minutes

Cake pan
Flat baking sheet, lined with waxed paper

Makes
35 cookies

Storage
Keep refrigerated in an airtight container for 1–2 weeks

Tea or coffee and pastries from your kitchen should always be accompanied by an afternoon visit from a dear friend.

Bienenstich

A particular family favorite, these delicious buttery fingers are covered with an almond toffee topping. The fresher they are, the better they taste.

INGREDIENTS

For the topping

7 tbsp (100g) butter

scant ½ cup (100g) granulated sugar

2 tbsp light brown sugar

2 tbsp milk

2 cups (250g) sliced almonds

For the base

½ cup (125g) unsalted butter

½ cup (125g) granulated sugar

1 egg

1 tsp finely grated lemon zest

1¼ cups (200g) all-purpose flour, sifted

1 tsp baking powder

1 For the topping, melt the butter in a medium-size pan. Stir in the granulated sugar, brown sugar, and the milk. Bring to a rapid boil, stirring all the time, then remove from the heat and stir in the sliced almonds, making sure that all the nuts are well coated with the toffee. Set aside and let cool slightly.

2 For the base, beat the butter and sugar together until pale and fluffy. Beat in the egg and lemon zest. Sift the flour and baking powder together. Gradually beat into the butter mixture until evenly mixed.

3 Spread the base mixture evenly into the prepared pan and lightly level the surface. Spoon on the almond topping and spread it out carefully.

4 Bake in the preheated oven for 35 minutes, or until golden. Remove from the oven and immediately cut into slices before the topping hardens. Let rest in the pan until cold. Remove from the pan and peel off the lining paper to serve.

Oven temperature
350°F/180°C

Baking time
35 minutes

Cake pan
9in (23cm) shallow, square pan, greased and lined

Makes
15 slices

Storage
Keep for 4–5 days

Ice Creams

Ices have been a passion in northern Italy for centuries. From there, Catherine de Medici's chefs introduced them to the French court in the 16th century. By the 17th century, the word had spread to England, brought by Italian chefs who were also opening cafés in Paris to sell ices and, later, ice creams. It was Italians, once again, who took ice cream to North America in the early 19th century. Today, ice cream is just as much a treat as ever, particularly when it is made at home with real cream, fresh eggs, and milk.

Chocolate Praline Ice Cream

An excellent chocolate ice cream to keep in the freezer, this has been given a crunchy texture by the addition of almond praline. If you prefer a smooth ice cream, omit the praline.

INGREDIENTS

3½oz (100g) praline (see page 30)
For the ice cream
6oz (180g) semisweet chocolate
2 cups (450ml) milk
5 egg yolks
½ cup (125g) superfine sugar
1¼ cups (300ml) heavy cream, lightly whipped

1 Make the whole praline recipe and store it ready for use. Melt the chocolate and set it aside to cool.

2 Bring the milk almost to a boil. Whisk the egg yolks with the sugar until thick and light, then whisk in the milk.

3 Return the mixture to the saucepan and continue to cook over low heat, stirring constantly with a wooden spoon, until the custard thickens enough to coat the spoon and leave a trail when your finger is drawn across the back of the spoon. Do not allow it to come near a simmer, or it will curdle.

4 Stir the chocolate into the custard and strain into a bowl. Chill until cool, then fold in the whipped cream. Freeze the mixture in an ice cream machine. Alternatively, put it in the freezer at the lowest setting until set around the sides and bottom. Take it out and beat vigorously, then return to the freezer. Repeat the process. Before the ice cream has set, stir in 3½oz (100g) of the praline and return to the freezer.

SERVING THE ICE CREAM
Serve the ice cream in chocolate baskets, and decorated with piped shapes. Add flecks of edible gold foil to the piped decoration.

Makes
4½ cups (1 liter);
6–8 servings

Freezing
2–3 months

In 1846 a New Jersey housewife named Nancy Johnson invented the first hand-cranked ice cream freezer. Enjoy a scoop tonight in her honor!

Melted chocolate pipes easily into decorative shapes

For a sparkling effect, add tiny pieces of edible gold foil

CHOCOLATE PRALINE ICE CREAM
This is a luxurious ice cream, based on an egg custard. Very satisfying served simply, it also lends itself to being turned into an extravagantly presented showstopper.

Elegantly piped chocolate patterns decorate the ice cream

Cheesecakes

Traditionally made for festive occasions, the first cheesecakes were simply soft cheeses perfumed with spices and flower waters, then wrapped in thin pastry cases and baked. Today baked cheesecakes are gloriously rich and made from farmer or cream cheeses, eggs, sugar, and flavorings. They should be dense without being cloying. Contemporary cheesecakes can also be fruity, cold-set, and refreshingly light confections.

Mango & Passion Fruit Cheesecake

This chilled cheesecake makes a stunning dinner-party dessert. The fruit gives both tempting color and intense and aromatic flavor to counterbalance the richness of the Italian soft cheese.

Special Ingredients

Fresh mango

Passion fruit

Kiwi fruit

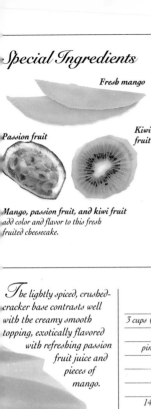

Mango, passion fruit, and kiwi fruit add color and flavor to this fresh fruited cheesecake.

Graham crackers *make a delicious base for cheesecakes and are easy to crush in a sealed plastic bag.*

Ground cinnamon *gives subtle flavor to the cracker base, and complements the flavor of the mango perfectly.*

Nutmeg *adds a warm spicy note. Grate it fresh for the recipe just before using.*

Apricot jam *subtly flavors and helps to bind the cracker crumb base.*

Gelatin *is sprinkled onto cold liquid, then gently heated until clear. It lightly sets the rich cheese filling.*

— Making the cheesecake —

The lightly spiced, crushed-cracker base contrasts well with the creamy smooth topping, exotically flavored with refreshing passion fruit juice and pieces of mango.

INGREDIENTS

For the base

3 cups (180g) crushed graham crackers
½ tsp ground cinnamon
pinch of freshly grated nutmeg
5 tbsp (75g) butter
1 tbsp apricot jam

For the filling

14oz (425g) canned or frozen mango slices
1½ tbsp unflavored gelatin
6 passion fruit
grated zest and juice of 1 orange
4 eggs, separated
⅔ cup (150g) granulated sugar
1 cup (200g) mascarpone cheese
1 cup (250ml) heavy cream, whipped

For the decoration

2 fresh mangoes, peeled and sliced
1–2 kiwi fruit, peeled and sliced
pulp from 1 passion fruit

1 For the base, mix the crackers and spices together. Melt the butter and the apricot jam. Mix into the crackers and then spoon into the prepared pan. Press evenly onto the bottom with a spoon, then chill.

2 For the filling, drain the canned mangoes and spoon 6 tablespoons (90ml) of the juice into a heatproof bowl. Sprinkle with the gelatin and let stand for 5 minutes. Sit the bowl in a pan of simmering water and let stand until clear. Remove and set aside.

3 Decorate the sides of the prepared pan with 5–6 of the mango slices. Roughly chop the remainder. Halve the passion fruit, scoop the pulp into a sieve, and press the juice into a bowl. Stir the orange zest and juice into the passion fruit juice with the chopped mango and dissolved gelatin.

4 Whisk the egg yolks and sugar together until thick and mousselike. Whisk in the mascarpone cheese. Stir in the fruit mixture and set aside until it starts to thicken and set.

5 Whisk the egg whites into soft peaks. Quickly fold the whipped cream into the setting cheese mixture, followed by the egg whites. Pour into the pan and chill for at least 5 hours, or until set.

6 Remove from the pan and transfer to a plate. Decorate the top with the mango and kiwi fruit slices. Spoon the passion fruit pulp into the center.

Cake pan
8½in (22cm) springform pan, greased lightly with vegetable oil and lined

Makes
10–12 slices

Storage
Keeps for 3 days

Warning
This recipe contains raw eggs

A light meal deserves a substantial dessert. The rich yet delicate texture of cheesecake is the perfect finishing touch for an appetite that is not fully satisfied.

Snacktime Chocolate

Homemade squares and small cakes are always greatly appreciated, few more so than the Brownies that feature here. They are among the easiest of squares to bake, and there are many variations on the basic recipe. Other recipes with the same virtues of being quick to make and delicious to eat are Chocolate Muffins and Bishop's Bread, a splendid chocolate tea bread. Other favorites are the choux pastry treats, Eclairs and Profiteroles, and meringues that have been given the full chocolate treatment.

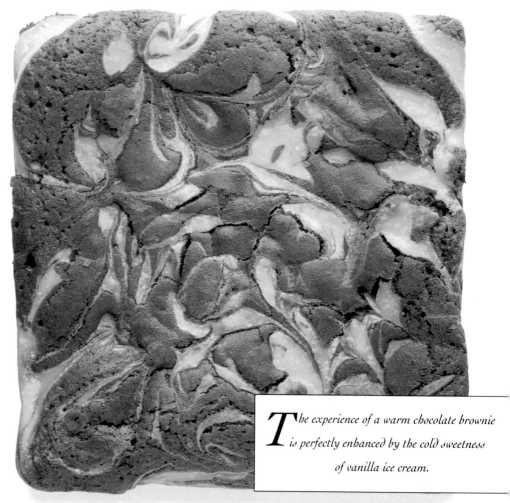

The experience of a warm chocolate brownie is perfectly enhanced by the cold sweetness of vanilla ice cream.

Swirls of chocolate: Marbled Brownies ready to cut into squares

Brownies

There must be hundreds of recipes for brownies, and this is one of the best. It has the added virtue of being quick to make. There is an easily made marbled variation, too, in which the walnuts are replaced by cream cheese.

INGREDIENTS

½ cup (125g) lightly salted butter

⅓ cup (45g) cocoa powder

2 eggs

1 cup (250g) superfine sugar

½ cup (60g) self-rising flour

¼ cup (90g) walnuts

1 Gently melt the butter in a small, heavy-based saucepan, then stir in the cocoa until blended and set aside.

2 Beat the eggs until light and fluffy. Gradually add the sugar and stir in the chocolate mixture. Sift the flour over the top and fold it into the mixture. Fold in the nuts.

3 Pour the mixture into the prepared pan and bake in the preheated oven for 30–35 minutes, or until just cooked through and springy to the touch. Brownies are at their best when moist, so be careful not to overbake them.

4 Cool the brownies in the pan. Turn it out and cut into squares. If desired, melt 2oz (60g) semisweet chocolate and spread over the cooled cake before cutting it into squares.

VARIATION
Marbled Brownies
For these, make the Brownies recipe to the end of step 2, replacing the walnuts with 1 teaspoon vanilla extract.

For the marbling, whisk together ¾ cup (180g) cream cheese, 1 egg, and ⅓ cup (90g) superfine sugar; sift ¼ cup (30g) self-rising flour over this mixture and fold in. Add 1 teaspoon vanilla extract.

Pour three-quarters of the basic brownie mixture into the prepared pan and spread the cream cheese mixture over it. Drop spoonfuls of the remaining brownie mixture on top, making swirls with a knife. Bake for 35–40 minutes, or until the top is springy to the touch.

 Oven temperature
350°F/180°C

 Baking time
30–35 minutes

 Baking pan
8in (20cm) square cake pan, lined

 Makes
16 squares

 Storage
Keep for 3–4 days in the refrigerator

Freezing
1–2 months, un-iced

Marbled Brownie

Blonde Brownies

These are a less rich version of the classic brownie, with a caramel flavor. Like all brownies, they firm up as they cool, so be careful not to overbake them. Cooling them in the pan helps keep them moist.

INGREDIENTS

⅓ cup (75g) granulated sugar

2 tbsp water

12 tbsp (180g) unsalted butter

1 cup (180g) light brown sugar

2 eggs, lightly beaten

1½ cups (200g) self-rising flour, sifted

⅛ tsp salt

¼ cup (90g) walnuts, chopped

3oz (90g) semisweet chocolate, chopped into pea-size pieces

1 Heat the granulated sugar gently in a small, heavy-based saucepan until the sugar melts and caramelizes. Swirl the pan when the sugar colors and take it off the heat when it becomes a dark caramel color. Add the water to the caramel at arm's length to avoid splashes.

2 Cream the butter, then beat in the brown sugar until the mixture is light and fluffy. Gradually add the eggs to the creamed ingredients. Stir in the caramel, heating gently to thin it if it has become too thick to pour readily.

3 Sift the flour and salt together and fold into the mixture. Fold in the walnuts and chocolate.

4 Turn the mixture into the prepared pan. Bake in the preheated oven for 40–45 minutes, or until a skewer inserted into the center comes out clean. Run a knife around the inside of the pan and let the cake cool for 10 minutes. Turn out and cut into squares.

 Oven temperature
350°F/180°C

 Baking time
40–45 minutes

 Baking pan
8in (20cm) square cake pan, lined

 Makes
16 squares

 Storage
Keep for 3–4 days in an airtight container

 Freezing
2 months

Cold Desserts

A refreshing lightness characterizes these cool desserts, which include mousses, elegant terrines, and smooth creams. A fine array of chocolates are mixed with memorable combinations of flavorings – white chocolate with limes or semisweet chocolate with rum or an orange liqueur, for example – providing both unusual and classical partnerships. In many recipes, coffee emphasizes the richness of the chocolate. Sauces, creams, and elegant decorations put the perfect finishing touch to every dessert.

Chocolate Velvet Mousse

This is a gloriously smooth mousse – hence its evocative name. It is elegant served simply with a light Crème Anglaise, but also makes an excellent base for more adventurous desserts.

INGREDIENTS

5oz (150g) bittersweet chocolate, melted
3 eggs, separated
5 tbsp (75g) unsalted butter, cut into small pieces
1 tbsp crème de cacao or Tia Maria or 2 tsp vanilla extract
1 egg white
pinch of salt
1 quantity Crème Anglaise (see page 30)
melted semisweet chocolate, to decorate

1 Melt the chocolate. While still hot, beat in the egg yolks, one at a time. Stir in the butter, and when the mixture is smooth, add the liqueur or vanilla extract.

2 Whisk all 4 egg whites with a pinch of salt until the whites form stiff peaks. Fold a heaping spoonful of the whites into the chocolate mixture to lighten it, then carefully fold in the remaining whites.

3 Turn the mixture into the dish, cover, and chill until it is set – about 4 hours.

4 To serve, pour Crème Anglaise onto individual dessert plates. Warm a serving spoon in hot water and then dip the spoon into the mousse to make an oval-shaped scoop. Put scoops, round side up, on the Crème Anglaise. To decorate, pipe lines of melted chocolate on top, using a toothpick to pull it into a pattern.

 Baking dish
8in (20cm) gratin or other shallow dish

Makes
6 servings

Storage
Keeps for 1 week, covered, in the refrigerator

✳ **Warning**
This recipe contains uncooked egg whites

Marbled Millefeuilles
(See below left)

VARIATION
Marbled Millefeuilles
Put spoonfuls of Chocolate Velvet Mousse between marbled plain and white chocolate waves, stacking them up as you would a layer cake.

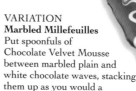

MARBLED MILLEFEUILLE sets creamy Chocolate Velvet Mousse between crisp waves of semisweet and white chocolate.

Chocolate waves are shaped over wooden-spoon handles

A cold dessert can be a year-round treat.

Chocolate Velvet Mousse spooned between chocolate waves 3in (7cm) square

Sauces & Fillings

Add a richly flavored chocolate filling to a cake or a smooth sauce to a dessert, and you immediately lift them out of the everyday into the luxury class. The chocolate sauce and fillings here are perfect with chocolate-based recipes, but would also add an extra dimension to recipes that do not contain chocolate. As with any chocolate recipe, the success of a chocolate sauce depends on the quality of the chocolate used. Always choose a chocolate with a high cocoa solid content and not too much sugar.

Almond Praline

Almond praline adds a sophisticated touch to layer cakes and ice cream.

INGREDIENTS

3½oz (100g) granulated sugar

3½oz (100g) shelled unblanched almonds

1 Put the nuts and sugar in a saucepan over a low heat.

2 Stir occasionally until the sugar is a deep golden color. Pour the praline onto an oiled baking sheet and spread out. Once cold, break into pieces and grind to the required consistency in a blender.

 Storage
Keeps for several weeks in an air-tight container at room temperature

Crème Anglaise

Crème Anglaise, a light soothing custard, is very good served with a variety of chocolate desserts. It is also the base for many ice creams. It has to be made with care to ensure that the egg yolks, which thicken the milk, do not curdle.

INGREDIENTS

1¼ cups (300ml) milk

½ vanilla bean, split lengthwise, or 1 tsp vanilla extract

3 egg yolks

2 tbsp superfine sugar

1 Bring the milk almost to the boil, with the vanilla bean, if you are using it.

2 Beat the egg yolks with the sugar until thick and light, then whisk in the hot milk. Return the mixture to the pan and cook over low heat, stirring constantly with a wooden spoon, until the cream thickens slightly. Do not allow the mixture to come near a simmer, or it will curdle.

3 Strain the mixture into a bowl and let it cool, when it will thicken more. Add the vanilla extract, if using, and refrigerate for several hours.

 Makes
1½ cups (350ml)

 Storage
Keeps 2–3 days in the refrigerator

Glacé Icing

This simple icing is best on light textured cakes and pastries, and is used while warm.

INGREDIENTS

7oz (200g) icing sugar, sifted

7–8 tsp boiling water

4 drops vanilla extract

1 Sift the icing sugar into a small bowl. Gradually stir in the boiling water until the mixture is smooth and coats the back of a spoon. Adjust accordingly with icing sugar or water. Stir in the vanilla extract.

2 Rest the bowl over a small pan of simmering water and leave for 1–2 minutes until warm. Use immediately.

To flavor the icing: omit the vanilla extract and substitute the following for the water:
Lemon: 7–8 tsp lemon juice.
Chocolate: Replace 1oz (30g) of the icing sugar with 1oz (30g) cocoa powder. Sift together and slowly add 7–8 tsp boiling water.

 Makes
Sufficient to cover the top and sides of an 8in (20cm) round cake.

 Storage
Keeps 1–2 days, covered, in the refrigerator

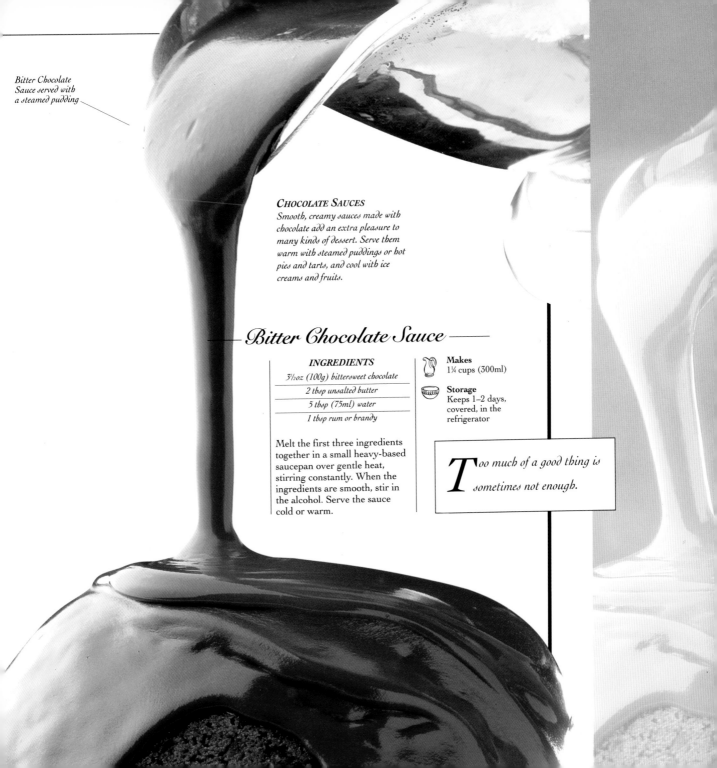

Bitter Chocolate Sauce served with a steamed pudding

CHOCOLATE SAUCES

Smooth, creamy sauces made with chocolate add an extra pleasure to many kinds of dessert. Serve them warm with steamed puddings or hot pies and tarts, and cool with ice creams and fruits.

— Bitter Chocolate Sauce —

INGREDIENTS

3½oz (100g) bittersweet chocolate
2 tbsp unsalted butter
5 tbsp (75ml) water
1 tbsp rum or brandy

Makes
1¼ cups (300ml)

Storage
Keeps 1–2 days, covered, in the refrigerator

Melt the first three ingredients together in a small heavy-based saucepan over gentle heat, stirring constantly. When the ingredients are smooth, stir in the alcohol. Serve the sauce cold or warm.

Too much of a good thing is sometimes not enough.

Basic Ingredients

Keep a selection of these basic ingredients so that you can bake whenever you wish. The more unusual ones are available from health food stores. Your cakes and cookies will taste delicious and look most appetizing if you choose only the best-quality produce and the freshest dairy goods. Do not store any ingredients in large quantities as they soon deteriorate; it is better to keep smaller amounts and replace them more often.

Flours, Leaveners, & Thickening Agents

The baking qualities of flours vary according to their ability to form gluten when moistened. Gluten sets when heated, trapping air in the mixture. The gluten in all-purpose flour gives a soft texture; potato starch and cornstarch give more structure.

All-purpose and self-rising flour: *All-purpose flour is used on its own in whisked and rich fruit cakes and cookies, or together with a leavening agent. Self-rising flour already includes some baking powder.*

Rye flour: *A whole-grain brown flour that gives a rich color and a delicious nutty taste to cakes and tea loaves.*

Potato starch: *Made from boiled, sieved, and dried potatoes, this produces a delicately textured cake.*

Points to Remember for Successful Baking:

Semolina flour: *Fine-grained, rich in protein and starch, this gives a good texture.*

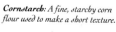

Cornstarch: *A fine, starchy corn flour used to make a short texture.*

Gelatin: *Gives a taste-free, firm set to soft cake fillings and cheesecakes.*

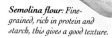

Matzo meal: *Crushed crumbs of unleavened crackers used in place of flour and as a thickener.*

Baking soda: *Acts as a leavening agent when combined with an acid such as lemon juice.*

Baking powder: *This reacts with moisture to produce carbon dioxide, which helps a cake to rise.*

Cream of tartar: *An acidic substance that stabilizes egg whites during beating.*

Sweeteners

Sugars and syrups affect the structure of
a cake and improve its texture,
color, and flavor. Store
in airtight containers
in a cool, dry place.

Superfine sugar: Best for
making meringues and fruit
desserts, because the fine
crystals dissolve and blend
quickly with other ingredients.

Golden syrup: Gives the
finished cake a moist texture.

Honey: Used for
centuries, a natural
sweetener enhancing
flavor and keeping
quality of cakes.

Maple syrup: This
natural sweetener has a
strong, distinctive flavor.

 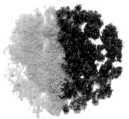 

Confectioners' sugar: A fine,
powdery sugar, ideal for icings and
fillings. It must be sifted before use.

Granulated and colored sugars:
Use granulated sugar for most
cakes; colored for decorating.

Light and dark brown sugars: Raw
cane sugars add moisture, color, and a
caramel flavor to cakes.

Raw sugar: Unrefined with a low
molasses content, this gives a good
flavor to fruit and spice cakes.

Dairy Produce

Store dairy products in
the refrigerator; butter
may be frozen. If not
fresh they will taint the
baking. Fresh dairy
products add a rich
flavor to good baking.

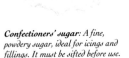

Heavy cream: Contains a high
percentage of fat, which allows it to be
whipped firmly without separating.

Cream or farmer cheese: Full-fat
cream cheese is richer and more
creamy. Farmer cheese is lower in
fat, drier, and slightly acidic.

Ricotta cheese: A slightly grainy,
low-fat soft cheese with a sweet taste.

   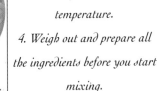

Eggs: Add flavor, color, and
lightness to a cake. Use large eggs
unless the recipe states otherwise.
Always use at room temperature.

Milk: Good for moistening and
loosening thick cake mixtures. Also
gives a softer crust to choux pastry.
Whole milk is most commonly used.

Sunflower or corn oil: For
rich moisture in some fruit
sponges and spiced cakes.

Butter: The distinctive flavor in
much baking. Use unsalted butter
for cakes unless otherwise stated.

*1. Choose a time when you can
work without distraction or
interruption.*

*2. Be sure that you have all
the ingredients required for
any recipe before you start.*

*3. Unless directed otherwise,
always use ingredients at room
temperature.*

*4. Weigh out and prepare all
the ingredients before you start
mixing.*

Enriching Ingredients

Nuts, dried fruit, and spices were used extensively in the general cuisine of ancient times. Today they are important for enriching cakes and pastries. Buy in small amounts as spices soon lose their pungency and nuts become rancid and bitter after 3–4 months. Dried fruit also spoils with time. Store in airtight containers in a cool, dry place.

Nuts & Dried Fruit

Almonds: *Available whole, ground, or sliced, almonds are sweet to taste.*

Pistachios: *Their distinctive green kernels add color and flavor. Use unsalted ones and blanch before use.*

Pine nuts: *The soft, oily-textured seed of the stone pine has a strong flavor that is enhanced by baking.*

Hazelnuts: *Toast first to bring out their rich flavor.*

Walnuts: *Rich in oil and protein, with an unmistakable flavor.*

Pecans: *Flavorful and rich, these nuts are ideal for fruit cakes.*

Coconut: *Freshly grated, it gives moisture to a cake. Thinly pared shavings make a pretty decoration.*

Golden raisins: *Produced from seedless green grapes. Add flavor by plumping in brandy before using.*

Figs: *Provide excellent fruity flavor with a seedy crunch. Buy them whole, remove the stems, and then cut by hand. They can be plumped up by soaking overnight in cold water.*

Dates: *A sun-dried fruit, these add moisture and sweet, rich flavor.*

Dark raisins: *Dried Muscatel grapes; seedless ones are the best.*

Dried cranberries: *Distinctive red berries with a piquant flavor.*

Dried apricots: *These soft, moist fruits may be plumped up before use.*

Flavorings & Spices

Instant coffee: An easy way to add rich coffee flavor.

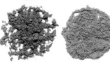

Cocoa powder and chocolate drink powder: Crushed from the "chocolate liquor" of dried, roasted cocoa beans.

Tiny seeds lie inside the bean

Vanilla bean and seeds: Add a sweet, mellow flavor. Make vanilla sugar by placing a bean in a jar of superfine sugar.

Dark rum: A strongly aromatic and richly flavored spirit distilled from sugar cane.

Brandy: Distilled from grapes, this spirit has a deep, mellow flavor.

Kirsch: A fiery eau de vie made from crushed fermented cherries.

Vanilla extract: Made by macerating crushed vanilla beans in alcohol.

Orange-flower water: Strongly perfumed distilled flower essence.

Nutmeg: This dried kernel imparts a warm, richly aromatic flavor to many spiced cakes. Best used freshly grated.

Whole nutmeg

Allspice: Also known as Jamaican pepper, this is sweet yet peppery.

Poppy seeds: Oily ripened seeds with a rich, nutty flavor.

Cinnamon: The dried bark or powder has a sweet, pungent, woody aroma.

> 5. The oven should be switched on before starting preparation and have reached the recommended baking temperature before use.

Cloves: Dried flower buds with a bitter, sharp flavor, these can be bought whole or in powder form.

Lemon and orange zest: Contain the essential flavoring oils.

Aniseed: Adds a distinctive, sweet, licorice-like flavor and can be bought as seed or a fine powder.

Buy pieces with smooth skin

Fresh ginger: Gives a sharp, hot, aromatic flavor.

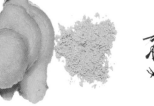

Powdered ginger: A highly concentrated, spicy and hot flavor; be careful to use the correct measure.

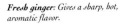

Saffron: One of the most expensive spices, prized for its color and taste.

Decorating Ingredients

Even the simplest decorations enhance the texture and flavor of a cake. Fresh and glacé fruits have the greatest visual appeal, with their tempting bright and colorful appearance.

Chocolate and coffee finishes give a wonderful dark, rich look to cakes, and subtly colored and finely flavored icings offer luxurious stylishness with little effort.

Fresh Fruit

> 6. The right baking tin is essential for a perfect result. Measure across the top of the tin from one inside wall to the other and disregard any other measurements stamped on the base of the tin.

Raspberries: *Sweet, juicy ruby red berries; the richer their color, the riper and more delicious they are.*

Grapes: *Select seedless varieties to embellish dessert-style cakes.*

Apples: *Choose crisp, shiny fruit with a good color. Firm, flavorful apples are best for tarts and cakes as they stay whole during baking.*

Blueberries: *Deep purple-skinned berries with dark green flesh, these are sweet yet tart and acidic, and blend well with other soft fruit.*

Strawberries: *These have a sweet, refreshing flavor. Choose firm, undamaged fruit with an even color and bright green stems.*

Oranges and lemons: *Strongly aromatic citrus fruit with a sweet acidic flavor. They add color and help neutralize any cloying sweetness in baking.*

Glacé Fruit

Glacé citron peel and clementines: *Buy good quality fruit that is soft-textured and not too sweet. Rinse off the excess sugar or syrup before using, if desired.*

Mixed chopped peel: *Precut orange and lemon peel is available.*

Angelica: *The crystallized stem of a large garden herb.*

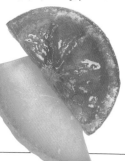

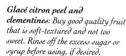

Natural and red glacé cherries: *Wash in warm water before baking to remove the sugary surface, then dry thoroughly on kitchen towels.*

Glacé pineapple: *Cut the whole circular slices to the size you require.*

Crystallized ginger: *Has a strong, sharp tang, so use sparingly.*

Preserves

Chestnut purée: The canned, unsweetened purée is good for use in cake fillings.

Seedless raspberry jam: Ideal as a sweet, distinctive filling in light sponge cakes.

Red currant jelly: Sharp, tangy, and very fruity.

Apricot jam: Adds a sharp, fruity flavor and helps bond icings to a cake's surface.

Marmalade: Use this citrus fruit preserve as a glaze for a glacé fruit decoration.

Strawberry jelly: Crystal clear with a tart sweetness.

Chocolate

Chocolate buttons: Small chocolate disks are ideal for children's cakes.

Chocolate coffee beans: Roasted coffee beans covered in chocolate.

Chocolate shapes make easy decorations

Chocolate: Semisweet chocolate containing 50–70% cocoa solids has the richest and best flavor for baking. Milk and white chocolate have less flavor but are good for decoration.

Chocolate thins: Slim squares of chocolate can be made by hand or bought from a candy store. They make good decorations for cakes, whole, halved, or cut into triangles.

Chocolate sticks: Narrow strips of flavored milk or semisweet chocolate are useful for decorating both children's party cakes and more sophisticated chocolate cakes.

> 7. The correct oven temperature is crucial for baking success. For perfect accuracy, it is best to check the temperature with an oven thermometer placed in the center of the oven before baking a cake.

Colorings

Be careful when using any food colorings as they are all very concentrated. Dip the tip of a fine skewer into the coloring, adding very gradually until the right shade is achieved. Remember that colors darken with time.

Red paste

Green liquid

Yellow liquid

Essential Tools & Baking Equipment

Here is a basic selection of the most useful equipment to have in the kitchen when you are baking cakes. A few more unusual items are also shown as they do make certain tasks much easier. When buying tools, always choose the best quality available: they last longer, are more reliable, and produce the best results. For successful baking, a complete set of measuring cups and spoons is essential, since ingredients must be measured carefully.

8. The baking time given in each recipe can only be used as a guide because every oven varies. Check a cake approximately five minutes before the end of the baking time by inserting a fine metal skewer into the center. The skewer should come out clean. If any mixture clings to it, bake for another five minutes.

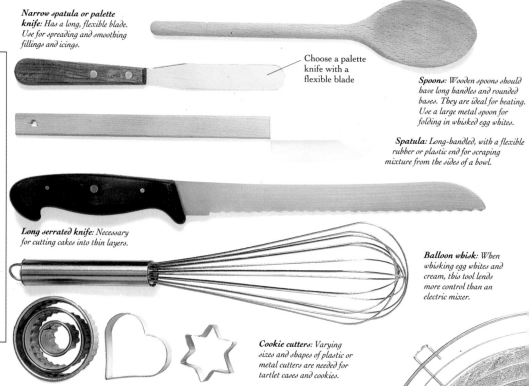

Narrow spatula or palette knife: *Has a long, flexible blade. Use for spreading and smoothing fillings and icings.*

Choose a palette knife with a flexible blade

Spoons: *Wooden spoons should have long handles and rounded bases. They are ideal for beating. Use a large metal spoon for folding in whisked egg whites.*

Spatula: *Long-handled, with a flexible rubber or plastic end for scraping mixture from the sides of a bowl.*

Long serrated knife: *Necessary for cutting cakes into thin layers.*

Balloon whisk: *When whisking egg whites and cream, this tool lends more control than an electric mixer.*

Cookie cutters: *Varying sizes and shapes of plastic or metal cutters are needed for tartlet cases and cookies.*

Rolling pin: *Must be completely smooth, at least 20in (50cm) long, and have straight, unshaped ends. Essential for rolling out pastry and sugar paste.*

Cake boards: *Lightweight boards covered in silver or gold paper are available in assorted sizes, shapes, and thicknesses for the assembly of celebration cakes.*

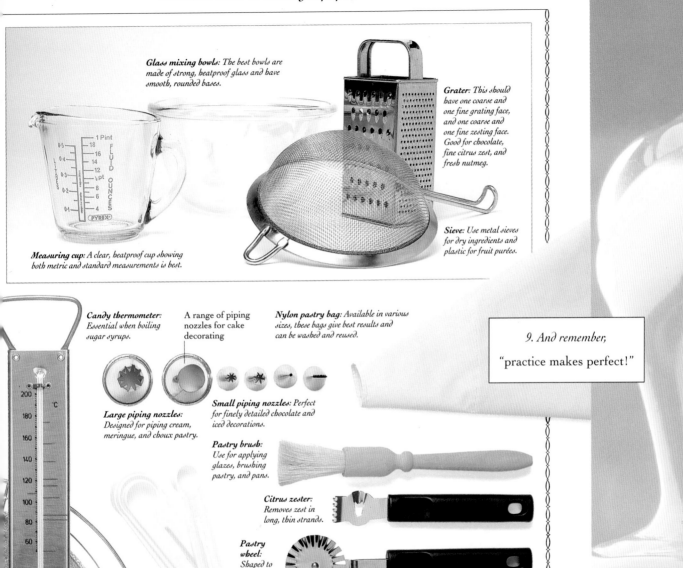

Glass mixing bowls: *The best bowls are made of strong, heatproof glass and have smooth, rounded bases.*

Grater: *This should have one coarse and one fine grating face, and one coarse and one fine zesting face. Good for chocolate, fine citrus zest, and fresh nutmeg.*

1 Pint
18
FLUID
16
14
12
½ pt
10
8
6
4
PYREX

Sieve: *Use metal sieves for dry ingredients and plastic for fruit purées.*

Measuring cup: *A clear, heatproof cup showing both metric and standard measurements is best.*

Candy thermometer: *Essential when boiling sugar syrups.*

A range of piping nozzles for cake decorating

Nylon pastry bag: *Available in various sizes, these bags give best results and can be washed and reused.*

9. And remember,

"practice makes perfect!"

Large piping nozzles: *Designed for piping cream, meringue, and choux pastry.*

Small piping nozzles: *Perfect for finely detailed chocolate and iced decorations.*

Pastry brush: *Use for applying glazes, brushing pastry, and pans.*

Citrus zester: *Removes zest in long, thin strands.*

Pastry wheel: *Shaped to cut pastry decoratively.*

Measuring spoons: *Accurate spoon measurements are possible with these. Must always be level unless otherwise stated.*

Wire racks: *Allow air to circulate beneath cooling cakes, dispersing any steam and preventing cakes from getting soggy and heavy.*

Vegetable peeler: *A swivel-bladed steel peeler is ideal for apples and pears and removing strips of lemon zest. You can also use it for making chocolate curls.*

200 °C
180
160
140
120
100
80
60

C.R.Gibson®
FINE GIFTS SINCE 1870

This book is based on *Ultimate Cake*, first published in Great Britain in 1996,
and *Ultimate Chocolate*, first published in Great Britain in 1997
by Dorling Kindersley Limited, London

Developed by Matthew A. Price, Nashville, Tennessee.

Published by C. R. Gibson®
C. R. Gibson® is a registered trademark of Thomas Nelson, Inc.
Norwalk, Connecticut 06856

Printed in Singapore by Star Standard

ISBN 0–7667–6162–2
UPC 082272–44983–1
GB4139

Acknowledgments

Dorling Kindersley would like to thank Catherine Atkinson for preparing some of the cakes that appear in the book; Nasim Mawji, Claire Benson, Jackie Jackson and Julia Pemberton Hellums for editorial assistance; Virginia Walter for design management; Vanessa Courtier for initial design work; Annette O'Sullivan and Kate L Scott for design assistance; Paul Wood and Suzy Dittmar for DTP design; Gilly Newman for illustrations. Props supplied by Tables Laid, China & Co., and Surfaces.

Picture Credits

Photography: Martin Cameron 32–33, 34–35, 36–37, 38–39; Dave King 1, 2–3, 4–5, 8–9, 16–17, 20–21, 24–25; Terry McCormick 12–13; Ian O'Leary 6–7, 10–11, 14–15, 18–19, 22–23, 26–27, 28–29, 30–31. Borders: Martin Cameron, Ian O'Leary.